**CONVENTION BETWEEN
THE GOVERNMENT OF THE UNITED STATES OF AMERICA
AND THE GOVERNMENT OF ICELAND
FOR THE AVOIDANCE OF DOUBLE TAXATION
AND THE PREVENTION OF FISCAL EVASION
WITH RESPECT TO TAXES ON INCOME**

The Government of the United States of America and the Government of Iceland,

desiring to conclude a Convention for the avoidance of double taxation and the prevention of

fiscal evasion with respect to taxes on income,

HAVE AGREED as follows:

ARTICLE 1
General Scope

1. This Convention shall apply only to persons who are residents of one or both of the Contracting States, except as otherwise provided in the Convention.

2. This Convention shall not restrict in any manner any benefit now or hereafter accorded:

    a) by the laws of either Contracting State; or

    b) by any other agreement between the Contracting States.

3.   a) Notwithstanding the provisions of subparagraph b) of paragraph 2:

        (i) the provisions of Article 24 (Mutual Agreement Procedure) of this Convention exclusively shall apply to any dispute concerning whether a measure is within the scope of this Convention, and the procedures under this Convention exclusively shall apply to that dispute; and

        (ii) unless the competent authorities determine that a taxation measure is not within the scope of this Convention, the non-discrimination obligations of this Convention exclusively shall apply with respect to that measure, except for such national treatment or most-favored-nation obligations as may apply to trade in goods under the General Agreement on Tariffs and Trade. No national treatment or most-favored-nation obligation under any other agreement shall apply with respect to that measure.

    b) For the purposes of this paragraph, a "measure" is a law, regulation, rule, procedure, decision, administrative action, or any similar provision or action.

4. Notwithstanding any provision of the Convention except paragraph 5 of this Article, a Contracting State may tax its residents (as determined under Article 4 (Resident)), and by reason of citizenship may tax its citizens, as if the Convention had not come into effect. Notwithstanding the other provisions of this Convention, a former citizen or long-term resident of the United States may, for the period of ten years following the loss of such status, be taxed in accordance with the laws of the United States.

5. The provisions of paragraph 4 shall not affect:

    a) the benefits conferred by a Contracting State under paragraph 2 of Article 9 (Associated Enterprises), paragraphs 2 and 4 of Article 17 (Pensions, Social Security, and Annuities), and Articles 22 (Relief from Double Taxation), 23 (Non-Discrimination), and 24 (Mutual Agreement Procedure); and

    b) the benefits conferred by a Contracting State under Articles 18 (Government Service), 19 (Students and Trainees), and 26 (Members of Diplomatic Missions and Consular Posts), upon individuals who are neither citizens of, nor have been admitted for permanent residence in, that State.

3

6. An item of income derived through an entity that is a partnership, trust or estate under the laws of either Contracting State shall be considered to be derived by a resident of a State to the extent that the item is treated for purposes of the taxation law of such Contracting State as the income of a resident, either in its hands or in the hands of its partners or beneficiaries.

ARTICLE 2
Taxes Covered

1. This Convention shall apply to taxes on income imposed on behalf of a Contracting State, irrespective of the manner in which they are levied.

2. There shall be regarded as taxes on income all taxes imposed on total income, on total capital, or on elements of income, including taxes on gains from the alienation of movable or immovable property (real property), taxes on the total amounts of wages or salaries paid by enterprises, but excluding social security taxes, as well as taxes on capital appreciation.

3. The existing taxes to which the Convention shall apply are:
    a) in Iceland:
        (i) the income taxes to the state *(tekjuskattar ríkissjóðs)*; and
        (ii) the income tax to the municipalities *(útsvar)*,
    (hereinafter referred to as "Icelandic tax");
    b) in the United States:
        (i) the Federal income taxes imposed by the Internal Revenue Code; and
        (ii) the Federal excise taxes imposed with respect to private foundations
    (hereinafter referred to as "United States tax").

4. The Convention shall apply also to any identical or substantially similar taxes that are imposed after the date of signature of the Convention in addition to, or in place of, the existing taxes. The competent authorities of the Contracting States shall notify each other of any significant changes that have been made in their respective taxation or other laws that significantly affect their obligations under this Convention.

ARTICLE 3
General Definitions

1. For the purposes of this Convention, unless the context otherwise requires:
    a) the term "Iceland" means Iceland and, when used in a geographical sense, means the territory of Iceland, including its territorial sea, and any area beyond the territorial sea within which Iceland, in accordance with international law, exercises jurisdiction or sovereign rights with respect to the sea bed, its subsoil and its superjacent waters, and their natural resources;

b) the term "United States" means the United States of America, and includes the states thereof and the District of Columbia; such term also includes the territorial sea thereof and the sea bed and subsoil of the submarine areas adjacent to that territorial sea, over which the United States exercises sovereign rights in accordance with international law; the term, however, does not include Puerto Rico, the Virgin Islands, Guam or any other United States possession or territory;

c) the term "person" includes an individual, an estate, a trust, a partnership, a company and any other body of persons;

d) the term "company" means any body corporate or any entity that is treated as a body corporate for tax purposes according to the laws of the state in which it is organized;

e) the term "enterprise" applies to the carrying on of any business;

f) the terms "enterprise of a Contracting State" and "enterprise of the other Contracting State" mean respectively an enterprise carried on by a resident of a Contracting State and an enterprise carried on by a resident of the other Contracting State;

g) the terms "a Contracting State" and "the other Contracting State" mean Iceland or the United States as the context requires;

h) the term "international traffic" means any transport by a ship or aircraft, except when such transport is solely between places in a Contracting State;

i) the term "competent authority" means:

(i) in the case of Iceland: the Minister of Finance or his authorized representative; and

(ii) in the case of the United States: the Secretary of the Treasury or his delegate;

j) the term "national" means:

(i) any individual possessing the nationality or citizenship of a Contracting State;

(ii) any legal person, partnership or association deriving its status as such from the laws in force in a Contracting State;

k) the term "business" includes the performance of professional services and of other activities of an independent character;

l) the term "pension scheme" means any plan, scheme, fund, trust or other arrangement established in a Contracting State that:

(i) is generally exempt from income taxation in that State; and

(ii) operates principally to administer or provide pension or retirement benefits or to earn income for the benefit of one or more such arrangements.

2. As regards the application of the Convention at any time by a Contracting State any term not defined therein shall, unless the context otherwise requires, or the competent

authorities agree to a common meaning pursuant to the provisions of Article 24 (Mutual Agreement Procedure), have the meaning that it has at that time under the law of that State for the purposes of the taxes to which the Convention applies, any meaning under the applicable tax laws of that State prevailing over a meaning given to the term under other laws of that State.

ARTICLE 4
Resident

1. For the purposes of this Convention, the term "resident of a Contracting State" means any person who, under the laws of that State, is liable to tax therein by reason of his domicile, residence, citizenship, place of management, place of incorporation or any other criterion of a similar nature, and also includes that State and any political subdivision or local authority thereof. This term, however, does not include any person who is liable to tax in that State in respect only of income from sources in that State or capital situated therein or of profits attributable to a permanent establishment in that State.

2. The term "resident of a Contracting State" includes:

a) a pension scheme;

b) a plan, scheme, fund, trust, company or other arrangement established in a Contracting State that is operated exclusively to administer or provide employee benefits and that, by reason of its nature as such, is generally exempt from income taxation in that State; and

c) an organization that is established exclusively for religious, charitable, scientific, artistic, cultural, or educational purposes and that is a resident of a Contracting State according to its laws,

notwithstanding that all or part of its income or gains may be exempt from tax under the domestic law of that State.

3. Where by reason of the provisions of paragraph 1 an individual is a resident of both Contracting States, then his status shall be determined as follows:

a) he shall be deemed to be a resident only of the State in which he has a permanent home available to him; if he has a permanent home available to him in both States, he shall be deemed to be a resident only of the State with which his personal and economic relations are closer (center of vital interests);

b) if the State in which he has his center of vital interests cannot be determined, or if he has not a permanent home available to him in either State, he shall be deemed to be a resident only of the State in which he has an habitual abode;

c) if he has an habitual abode in both States or in neither of them, he shall be deemed to be a resident only of the State of which he is a national;

d) if he is a national of both States or of neither of them, the competent authorities of the Contracting States shall settle the question by mutual agreement.

4. Where by reason of the provisions of paragraphs 1 and 2 of this Article a person other than an individual is a resident of both Contracting States, the competent authorities of the Contracting States shall endeavor to determine by mutual agreement the mode of application of this Convention to that person. If the competent authorities do not reach such an agreement, that person shall not be entitled to claim any benefit provided by this Convention, except those provided by Article 23 (Non-Discrimination) and Article 24 (Mutual Agreement Procedure).

ARTICLE 5
Permanent Establishment

1. For the purposes of this Convention, the term "permanent establishment" means a fixed place of business through which the business of an enterprise is wholly or partly carried on.

2. The term "permanent establishment" includes especially:

a) a place of management;

b) a branch;

c) an office;

d) a factory;

e) a workshop; and

f) a mine, an oil or gas well, a quarry or any other place of extraction of natural resources.

3. A building site or construction or installation project, or an installation or drilling rig or ship used for the exploration of natural resources constitutes a permanent establishment only if it lasts or the activity continues for more than twelve months.

4. Notwithstanding the preceding provisions of this Article, the term "permanent establishment" shall be deemed not to include:

a) the use of facilities solely for the purpose of storage, display or delivery of goods or merchandise belonging to the enterprise;

b) the maintenance of a stock of goods or merchandise belonging to the enterprise solely for the purpose of storage, display or delivery;

c) the maintenance of a stock of goods or merchandise belonging to the enterprise solely for the purpose of processing by another enterprise;

d) the maintenance of a fixed place of business solely for the purpose of purchasing goods or merchandise, or of collecting information for the enterprise;

e) the maintenance of a fixed place of business solely for the purpose of carrying on, for the enterprise, any other activity of a preparatory or auxiliary character;

f) the maintenance of a fixed place of business solely for any combination of activities mentioned in subparagraphs a) to e), provided that the overall activity of the fixed place of business resulting from this combination is of a preparatory or auxiliary character.

5. Notwithstanding the provisions of paragraphs 1 and 2, where a person -- other than an agent of an independent status to whom paragraph 6 applies -- is acting on behalf of an enterprise and has, and habitually exercises, in a Contracting State an authority to conclude contracts in the name of the enterprise, that enterprise shall be deemed to have a permanent establishment in that State in respect of any activities which that person undertakes for the enterprise, unless the activities of such person are limited to those mentioned in paragraph 4 which, if exercised through a fixed place of business, would not make this fixed place of business a permanent establishment under the provisions of that paragraph.

6. An enterprise shall not be deemed to have a permanent establishment in a Contracting State merely because it carries on business in that State through a broker, general commission agent or any other agent of an independent status, provided that such persons are acting in the ordinary course of their business as independent agents.

7. The fact that a company which is a resident of a Contracting State controls or is controlled by a company which is a resident of the other Contracting State, or which carries on business in that other State (whether through a permanent establishment or otherwise), shall not constitute either company a permanent establishment of the other.

ARTICLE 6
Income from Immovable Property (Real Property)

1. Income derived by a resident of a Contracting State from immovable property (real property), including income from agriculture or forestry, situated in the other Contracting State may be taxed in that other State.

2. The term "immovable property (real property)" shall have the meaning which it has under the law of the Contracting State in which the property in question is situated. The term shall in any case include property accessory to immovable property (real property), livestock and equipment used in agriculture and forestry, rights to which the provisions of general law respecting landed property apply, usufruct of immovable property (real property) and rights to variable or fixed payments as consideration for the working of, or the right to work, mineral deposits, sources and other natural resources; ships, boats and aircraft shall not be regarded as immovable property (real property).

3. The provisions of paragraph 1 shall apply to income derived from the direct use, letting or use in any other form of immovable property (real property).

4. The provisions of paragraphs 1 and 3 shall also apply to the income from immovable property (real property) of an enterprise.

ARTICLE 7
Business Profits

1. The profits of an enterprise of a Contracting State shall be taxable only in that State unless the enterprise carries on business in the other Contracting State through a permanent establishment situated therein. If the enterprise carries on business as aforesaid, the profits of the enterprise may be taxed in the other State but only so much of them as is attributable to that permanent establishment.

2. Subject to the provisions of paragraph 3 of this Article, where an enterprise of a Contracting State carries on business in the other Contracting State through a permanent establishment situated therein, there shall in each Contracting State be attributed to that permanent establishment the business profits that it might be expected to make if it were a distinct and separate enterprise engaged in the same or similar activities under the same or similar conditions and dealing wholly independently with the enterprise of which it is a permanent establishment. For this purpose, the business profits to be attributed to the permanent establishment shall include only the profits derived from the assets used, risks assumed and activities performed by the permanent establishment.

3. In determining the profits of a permanent establishment, there shall be allowed as deductions expenses which are incurred for the purposes of the permanent establishment, including executive and general administrative expenses so incurred, whether in the State in which the permanent establishment is situated or elsewhere.

4. No profits shall be attributed to a permanent establishment by reason of the mere purchase by that permanent establishment of goods or merchandise for the enterprise.

5. For the purposes of the preceding paragraphs, the profits to be attributed to the permanent establishment shall be determined by the same method year by year unless there is good and sufficient reason to the contrary.

6. Where profits include items of income which are dealt with separately in other Articles of this Convention, then the provisions of those Articles shall not be affected by the provisions of this Article.

7. In applying this Article, paragraph 6 of Article 10 (Dividends), paragraph 3 of Article 11 (Interest), paragraph 4 of Article 12 (Royalties), paragraph 3 of Article 13 (Capital Gains) and paragraph 2 of Article 20 (Other Income), any income or gain attributable to a permanent establishment during its existence is taxable in the Contracting State where such permanent establishment is situated even if the payments are deferred until such permanent establishment has ceased to exist.

ARTICLE 8
Shipping and Air Transport

1. Profits of an enterprise of a Contracting State from the operation of ships or aircraft in international traffic shall be taxable only in that State.

2. For the purposes of this Article, profits from the operation of ships or aircraft include profits derived from the rental of ships or aircraft on a full (time or voyage) basis. They also include profits from the rental of ships or aircraft on a bareboat basis if such ships or aircraft are operated in international traffic by the lessee, or if the rental income is incidental to profits from the operation of ships or aircraft in international traffic. Profits derived by an enterprise from the inland transport of property or passengers within either Contracting State shall be treated as profits from the operation of ships or aircraft in international traffic if such transport is undertaken as part of international traffic.

3. Profits of an enterprise of a Contracting State from the use, maintenance, or rental of containers (including trailers, barges, and related equipment for the transport of containers) used in international traffic shall be taxable only in that State.

4. The provisions of paragraphs 1 and 3 shall also apply to profits from the participation in a pool, a joint business or an international operating agency.

ARTICLE 9
Associated Enterprises

1. Where

a) an enterprise of a Contracting State participates directly or indirectly in the management, control or capital of an enterprise of the other Contracting State, or

b) the same persons participate directly or indirectly in the management, control or capital of an enterprise of a Contracting State and an enterprise of the other Contracting State,

and in either case conditions are made or imposed between the two enterprises in their commercial or financial relations which differ from those which would be made between independent enterprises, then any profits which would, but for those conditions, have accrued to one of the enterprises, but, by reason of those conditions, have not so accrued, may be included in the profits of that enterprise and taxed accordingly.

2. Where a Contracting State includes in the profits of an enterprise of that State --and taxes accordingly -- profits on which an enterprise of the other Contracting State has been charged to tax in that other State and the other Contracting State agrees that the profits so included are profits which would have accrued to the enterprise of the first-mentioned State if the conditions made between the two enterprises had been those which would have been made between independent enterprises, then that other State shall make an appropriate adjustment to the amount of the tax charged therein on those profits. In determining such adjustment, due

regard shall be had to the other provisions of this Convention and the competent authorities of the Contracting States shall if necessary consult each other.

ARTICLE 10
Dividends

1. Dividends paid by a company which is a resident of a Contracting State to a resident of the other Contracting State may be taxed in that other State.

2. However, such dividends may also be taxed in the Contracting State of which the company paying the dividends is a resident and according to the laws of that State, but if the beneficial owner of the dividends is a resident of the other Contracting State, the tax so charged shall not exceed:

a) 5 per cent of the gross amount of the dividends if the beneficial owner is a company which holds directly at least 10 per cent of the share capital of the company paying the dividends;

b) 15 per cent of the gross amount of the dividends in all other cases.

This paragraph shall not affect the taxation of the company in respect of the profits out of which the dividends are paid.

3. Subparagraph a) of paragraph 2 shall not apply in the case of dividends paid by a Regulated Investment Company (RIC) or a Real Estate Investment Trust (REIT). In the case of dividends paid by a RIC, subparagraph b) of paragraph 2 shall apply. In the case of dividends paid by a REIT, subparagraph b) of paragraph 2 also shall not apply unless:

a) the beneficial owner of the dividends is an individual holding an interest of not more than 10 percent in the REIT;

b) the dividends are paid with respect to a class of stock that is publicly traded and the beneficial owner of the dividends is a person holding an interest of not more than 5 percent of any class of the REIT's stock; or

c) the beneficial owner of the dividends is a person holding an interest of not more than 10 percent in the REIT and the REIT is diversified.

The rules of this paragraph shall also apply to dividends paid by companies resident in Iceland that are similar to the United States companies referred to in this paragraph. Whether companies that are residents of Iceland are similar to the United States companies referred to in this paragraph will be determined by mutual agreement of the competent authorities.

4. Notwithstanding paragraphs 2 or 3, dividends shall not be taxed in the Contracting State of which the company paying the dividends is a resident if the beneficial owner of the dividends is resident in the other Contracting State and is described in subparagraph a) or b) of paragraph 2 of Article 4 (Resident), provided that such dividends are not derived from the carrying on of a business, directly or indirectly, by such pension scheme or employee benefit organization.

5. For purposes of this Article, the term "dividends" means income from shares or other rights, not being debt-claims, participating in profits, as well as income that is subjected to the same taxation treatment as income from shares under the laws of the State of which the payer is a resident.

6. The provisions of paragraphs 1 through 4 shall not apply if the beneficial owner of the dividends, being a resident of a Contracting State, carries on business in the other Contracting State of which the company paying the dividends is a resident, through a permanent establishment situated therein and the holding in respect of which the dividends are paid is effectively connected with such permanent establishment. In such case the provisions of Article 7 (Business Profits) shall apply.

7. A Contracting State may not impose any tax on dividends paid by a resident of the other State, except insofar as the dividends are paid to a resident of the first-mentioned State or the dividends are attributable to a permanent establishment, nor may it impose tax on a corporation's undistributed profits, except as provided in paragraph 8, even if the dividends paid or the undistributed profits consist wholly or partly of profits or income arising in that State.

8. A company that is a resident of one of the States and that has a permanent establishment in the other State or that is subject to tax in the other State on a net basis on its income that may be taxed in the other State under Article 6 (Income from Immovable Property (Real Property)) or under paragraph 1 of Article 13 (Capital Gains) may be subject in that other State to a tax in addition to the tax allowable under the other provisions of this Convention. Such tax, however, may be imposed on only the portion of the business profits of the company attributable to the permanent establishment and the portion of the income referred to in the preceding sentence that is subject to tax under Article 6 or under paragraph 1 of Article 13 that, in the case of the United States, represents the dividend equivalent amount of such profits or income and, in the case of Iceland, is an amount that is analogous to the dividend equivalent amount.

9. The tax referred to in paragraph 8 may not be imposed at a rate in excess of the rate specified in subparagraph 2 a).

ARTICLE 11
Interest

1. Interest arising in a Contracting State and beneficially owned by a resident of the other Contracting State shall be taxable only in that other State.

2. The term "interest" as used in this Article means income from debt-claims of every kind, whether or not secured by mortgage and whether or not carrying a right to participate in the debtor's profits, and in particular, income from government securities and income from bonds or debentures, including premiums and prizes attaching to such securities, bonds or

debentures, and all other income that is subjected to the same taxation treatment as income from money lent by the taxation law of the Contracting State in which the income arises. Income dealt with in Article 10 (Dividends) and penalty charges for late payment shall not be regarded as interest for the purpose of this Article.

3. The provisions of paragraph 1 shall not apply if the beneficial owner of the interest, being a resident of a Contracting State, carries on business in the other Contracting State in which the interest arises, through a permanent establishment situated therein and the debt-claim in respect of which the interest is paid is effectively connected with such permanent establishment. In such case the provisions of Article 7 (Business Profits) shall apply.

4. Where, by reason of a special relationship between the payer and the beneficial owner or between both of them and some other person, the amount of the interest, having regard to the debt-claim for which it is paid, exceeds the amount which would have been agreed upon by the payer and the beneficial owner in the absence of such relationship, the provisions of this Article shall apply only to the last-mentioned amount. In such case, the excess part of the payments shall remain taxable according to the laws of each Contracting State, due regard being had to the other provisions of this Convention.

5. Notwithstanding the provisions of paragraph 1:

a) interest paid by a resident of a Contracting State and that is determined with reference to receipts, sales, income, profits or other cash flow of the debtor or a related person, to any change in the value of any property of the debtor or a related person or to any dividend, partnership distribution or similar payment made by the debtor to a related person also may be taxed in the Contracting State in which it arises, and according to the laws of that State, but if the beneficial owner is a resident of the other Contracting State, the gross amount of the interest may be taxed at a rate not exceeding the rate prescribed in subparagraph b) of paragraph 2 of Article 10 (Dividends); and

b) interest that is an excess inclusion with respect to a residual interest in a real estate mortgage investment conduit may be taxed by each State in accordance with its domestic law.

ARTICLE 12
Royalties

1. Royalties arising in a Contracting State and beneficially owned by a resident of the other Contracting State may be taxed only in that other State.

2. Notwithstanding the provisions of paragraph 1, such royalties may also be taxed in the Contracting State in which they arise if they constitute consideration for the use of, or the right to use

a) a trademark and any information concerning industrial, commercial or scientific experience provided in connection with a rental or franchise agreement that includes rights to use a trademark, or

b) a motion picture film or work on film or videotape or other means of reproduction for use in connection with television,

however the tax so charged shall not exceed 5 percent of the gross amount of the royalties.

3. The term "royalties" as used in this Article means payments of any kind received as a consideration for the use of, or the right to use, any copyright of literary, artistic, scientific or other work (including computer software, and cinematographic films), any patent, trade mark, design or model, plan, secret formula or process, or for information concerning industrial, commercial or scientific experience.

4. The provisions of paragraphs 1, 2 and 3 shall not apply if the beneficial owner of the royalties, being a resident of a Contracting State, carries on business in the other Contracting State in which the royalties arise, through a permanent establishment situated therein and the right or property in respect of which the royalties are paid is effectively connected with such permanent establishment. In such case the provisions of Article 7 (Business Profits) shall apply.

5. For the purposes of this Article,

a) Royalties shall be deemed to arise in a Contracting State when the payer is a resident of that State. Where, however, the person paying the royalties, whether he is a resident of a Contracting State or not, has in a State a permanent establishment in connection with which the obligation to pay the royalties was incurred, and such royalties are borne by such permanent establishment, then such royalties shall be deemed to arise in the State in which the permanent establishment is situated and not in any other State of which the payer is a resident;

b) Where subparagraph a) does not operate to treat royalties as arising in either Contracting State, and the royalties are for the use of, or the right to use, in one of the Contracting States, any property or right described in paragraph 3, the royalties shall be deemed to arise in that State.

6. Where, by reason of a special relationship between the payer and the beneficial owner or between both of them and some other person, the amount of the royalties, having regard to the use, right or information for which they are paid, exceeds the amount which would have been agreed upon by the payer, and the beneficial owner in the absence of such relationship, the provisions of this Article shall apply only to the last-mentioned amount. In such case, the excess part of the payments shall remain taxable according to the laws of each Contracting State, due regard being had to the other provisions of this Convention.

ARTICLE 13
Capital Gains

1. Gains derived by a resident of a Contracting State from the alienation of immovable property (real property) situated in the other Contracting State may be taxed in that other State.

2. For the purposes of this Article the term "immovable property (real property) situated in the other Contracting State" shall include:

a) immovable property (real property) referred to in Article 6 (Income from Immovable Property (Real Property));

b) rights to assets to be produced by the exploration or exploitation of the sea bed and sub-soil of that other State and their natural resources, including rights to interests in or the benefit of such assets;

c) where that other State is the United States, a United States real property interest; and

d) where that other State is Iceland,

(i) shares, including rights to acquire shares, other than shares in which there is regular trading on a stock exchange, deriving their value or the greater part of their value directly or indirectly from immovable property (real property) situated in Iceland; and

(ii) an interest in a partnership or trust to the extent that the assets of the partnership or trust consist of immovable property (real property) situated in Iceland, or of shares referred to in clause i) of this subparagraph.

3. Gains from the alienation of movable property forming part of the business property of a permanent establishment which an enterprise of a Contracting State has in the other Contracting State and gains from the alienation of such a permanent establishment (alone or with the whole enterprise) may be taxed in that other State.

4. Gains derived by an enterprise of a Contracting State from the alienation of ships, aircraft, or containers operated or used in international traffic or personal property pertaining to the operation or use of such ships, aircraft, or containers shall be taxable only in that State.

5. Gains from the alienation of any property other than that referred to in the preceding paragraphs shall be taxable only in the Contracting State of which the alienator is a resident.

6. The provisions of paragraph 5 shall not affect the right of each of the Contracting States to levy according to its own law a tax on gains from the alienation of shares or rights in a company, the capital of which is wholly or partly divided into shares and which under the laws of that State is a resident of that State, derived by an individual who is a resident of the other Contracting State and has been a resident of the first-mentioned State in the course of the last five years preceding the alienation of the shares or rights.

ARTICLE 14
Income from Employment

1. Subject to the provisions of Articles 15 (Directors' Fees), 17 (Pensions, Social Security, and Annuities), and 18 (Government Service), salaries, wages and other similar remuneration derived by a resident of a Contracting State in respect of an employment shall be taxable only in that State unless the employment is exercised in the other Contracting State. If the employment is so exercised, such remuneration as is derived therefrom may be taxed in that other State.

2. Notwithstanding the provisions of paragraph 1, remuneration derived by a resident of a Contracting State in respect of an employment exercised in the other Contracting State shall be taxable only in the first-mentioned State if:

a) the recipient is present in the other State for a period or periods not exceeding in the aggregate 183 days in any twelve-month period commencing or ending in the fiscal year or the taxable year concerned, and

b) the remuneration is paid by, or on behalf of, an employer who is not a resident of the other State, and

c) the remuneration is not borne by a permanent establishment which the employer has in the other State.

3. Notwithstanding the preceding provisions of this Article, remuneration described in paragraph 1 that is derived by a resident of a Contracting State in respect of an employment as a member of the regular complement of a ship or aircraft operated in international traffic shall be taxable only in that State.

ARTICLE 15
Directors' Fees

Directors' fees and other similar payments derived by a resident of a Contracting State in his capacity as a member of the board of directors of a company which is a resident of the other Contracting State may be taxed in that other State.

ARTICLE 16
Artistes and Sportsmen

1. Income derived by a resident of a Contracting State as an entertainer, such as a theater, motion picture, radio, or television artiste, or a musician, or as a sportsman, from his personal activities as such exercised in the other Contracting State, which income would be exempt from tax in that other Contracting State under the provisions of Articles 7 (Business Profits) and 14 (Income from Employment) may be taxed in that other State, except where the amount of the gross receipts derived by such entertainer or sportsman, including expenses

reimbursed to him, or borne on his behalf, from such activities does not exceed twenty thousand United States dollars ($20,000) or its equivalent in Icelandic kronur for the taxable year concerned.

2. Where income in respect of activities exercised by an entertainer or a sportsman in his capacity as such accrues not to the entertainer or sportsman himself but to another person, that income, notwithstanding the provisions of Article 7 (Business Profits), may be taxed in the Contracting State in which the activities of the entertainer or sportsman are exercised, unless such other person establishes that neither the entertainer or sportsman nor persons related thereto participate directly or indirectly in the profits of that other person in any manner, including the receipt of deferred remuneration, bonuses, fees, dividends, partnership distributions, or other distributions.

ARTICLE 17
Pensions, Social Security, and Annuities

1. Subject to the provisions of paragraph 2 of Article 18 (Government Service), pensions and other similar remuneration paid to a resident of a Contracting State in consideration of past employment shall be taxable only in that State.

2. Notwithstanding the provisions of paragraph 1, payments made by a Contracting State under provisions of the social security or similar legislation of that State to a resident of the other Contracting State or to a citizen of the United States shall be taxable only in the first-mentioned State.

3. Annuities derived and beneficially owned by an individual resident of a Contracting State shall be taxable only in that State. The term "annuities" as used in this paragraph means a stated sum paid periodically at stated times during a specified number of years, under an obligation to make the payments in return for adequate and full consideration (other than services rendered).

4. Where a resident of a Contracting State is a beneficiary of a pension scheme resident in the other Contracting State, income earned but not distributed by the pension scheme may be taxed in the first-mentioned State only at such time as and, subject to paragraph 1, to the extent that a distribution is made from the pension scheme.

ARTICLE 18
Government Service

1.   a) Salaries, wages and other similar remuneration, other than a pension, paid from the public funds of a Contracting State or a political subdivision or a local authority thereof to an individual in respect of services rendered to that State or

subdivision or authority in the discharge of functions of a governmental nature shall be taxable only in that State.

b) However, such salaries, wages and other similar remuneration shall be taxable only in the other Contracting State if the services are rendered in that State and the individual is a resident of that State who:

(i) is a national of that State; or

(ii) did not become a resident of that State solely for the purpose of rendering the services.

2. a) Any pension paid by, or out of funds created by, a Contracting State or a political subdivision or a local authority thereof to an individual in respect of services rendered to that State or subdivision or authority in the discharge of functions of a governmental nature (other than a payment to which paragraph 2 of Article 17 (Pensions, Social Security, and Annuities) applies) shall be taxable only in that State.

b) However, such pension shall be taxable only in the other Contracting State if the individual is a resident of, and a national of, that State.

3. The provisions of Articles 14 (Income from Employment), 15 (Directors' Fees), 16 (Artistes and Sportsmen), and 17 (Pensions, Social Security, and Annuities) shall apply to salaries, wages and other similar remuneration and to pensions in respect of services rendered in connection with a business carried on by a Contracting State or a political subdivision or a local authority thereof.

ARTICLE 19
Students and Trainees

1. a) An individual who is a resident of one of the Contracting States at the time he becomes temporarily present in the other Contracting State and who is temporarily present in that other Contracting State for the primary purpose of:

(i) studying at a university or other recognized educational institution in that other Contracting State, or

(ii) securing training required to qualify him to practice a profession or professional specialty, or

(iii) studying or doing research as a recipient of a grant, allowance, or award from a governmental, religious, charitable, scientific, literary, or educational organization,

shall be exempt from tax by that other Contracting State with respect to amounts described in subparagraph b) for a period not exceeding 5 taxable years from the date of his arrival in that other Contracting State.

b) The amounts referred to in subparagraph a) are:

(i) gifts from abroad for the purpose of his maintenance, education, study, research, or training;

(ii) the grant, allowance, or award; and

(iii) income from personal services performed in that other Contracting State in an amount not in excess of nine thousand United States dollars ($9,000) or its equivalent in Icelandic kronur for any taxable year.

2. An individual who is a resident of one of the Contracting States at the time he becomes temporarily present in the other Contracting State and who is temporarily present in that other Contracting State as an employee of, or under Contract with, a resident of the first-mentioned Contracting State, for the primary purpose of:

a) acquiring technical, professional, or business experience from a person other than that resident of the first-mentioned Contracting State or other than a person related to such resident, or

b) studying at a university or other recognized educational institution in that other Contracting State,

shall be exempt from tax by that other Contracting State for a period of 12 consecutive months with respect to his income from personal services in an aggregate amount not in excess of nine thousand United States dollars ($9,000) or its equivalent in Icelandic kronur.

3. An individual who is a resident of one of the Contracting States at the time he becomes temporarily present in the other Contracting State and who is temporarily present in that other Contracting State for a period not exceeding 1 year, as a participant in a program sponsored by the Government of that other Contracting State, for the primary purpose of training, research, or study, shall be exempt from tax by that other Contracting State with respect to his income from personal services in respect of such training, research, or study performed in that other Contracting State in an aggregate amount not in excess of nine thousand United States dollars ($9,000) or its equivalent in Icelandic kronur.

ARTICLE 20
Other Income

1. Items of income beneficially owned by a resident of a Contracting State, wherever arising, not dealt with in the foregoing Articles of this Convention shall be taxable only in that State.

2. The provisions of paragraph 1 shall not apply to income, other than income from immovable property (real property) as defined in paragraph 2 of Article 6 (Income from Immovable Property (Real Property)), if the beneficial owner of such income, being a resident of a Contracting State, carries on business in the other Contracting State through a permanent establishment situated therein and the right or property in respect of which the income is paid is

effectively connected with such permanent establishment. In such case the provisions of Article 7 (Business Profits) shall apply.

ARTICLE 21
Limitation on Benefits

1. A resident of a Contracting State shall be entitled to benefits otherwise accorded to residents of a Contracting State by this Convention only to the extent provided in this Article.

2. A resident of a Contracting State shall be entitled to all the benefits of this Convention if the resident is:

    a) an individual;

    b) a Contracting State or any political subdivision or local authority thereof;

    c) a company if,

        (i) its principal class of shares is regularly traded on one or more recognized stock exchanges, and either

            A) its principal class of shares is primarily traded on a recognized stock exchange located in the Contracting State of which the company is a resident; or

            B) the company's primary place of management and control is in the Contracting State of which it is a resident; or

        (ii) at least 50 percent of the aggregate vote and at least 50 percent of the aggregate value of the shares in the company are owned directly or indirectly by five or fewer companies entitled to benefits under clause (i) of this subparagraph, provided that, in the case of indirect ownership, each intermediate owner is a resident of either Contracting State;

    d) a person described in paragraph 2 of Article 4 (Resident) of this Convention, provided that, in the case of a person described in subparagraph a) or subparagraph b) of that paragraph, more than 50 percent of the person's beneficiaries, members or participants are individuals resident in either Contracting State; or

    e) a person other than an individual, if:

        (i) on at least half the days of the taxable year at least 50 percent of each class of shares or other beneficial interests in the person is owned, directly or indirectly, by residents of that State that are entitled to the benefits of this Convention under subparagraph a), subparagraph b), clause (i) of subparagraph c), or subparagraph d) of this paragraph, provided that, in the case of indirect ownership, each intermediate owner is a resident of that Contracting State; and

        (ii) less than 50 percent of the person's gross income for the taxable year, as determined in the person's State of residence, is paid or accrued, directly or indirectly, to persons who are not residents of either Contracting

State entitled to the benefits of this Convention under subparagraph a), subparagraph b), clause (i) of subparagraph c), or subparagraph d) of this paragraph in the form of payments that are deductible for purposes of the taxes covered by this Convention in the person's State of residence (but not including arm's length payments in the ordinary course of business for services or tangible property and payments in respect of financial obligations to a bank, provided that where such a bank is not a resident of a Contracting State such payment is attributable to a permanent establishment of that bank located in one of the Contracting States).

3.   a) A company that is a resident of a Contracting State shall also be entitled to the benefits of the Convention if:

(i) at least 95 percent of the aggregate vote and at least 95 percent of the value of all its shares is owned, directly or indirectly, by seven or fewer persons that are residents of Member States of the European Union, or of the European Economic Area, or parties to the North American Free Trade Agreement or the European Free Trade Agreement that, in any case, meet the requirements of subparagraph b), or any combination thereof; and

(ii) less than 50 percent of the company's gross income for the taxable year is paid or accrued, in the form of deductible payments, directly or indirectly, to persons who are not residents of Member States of the European Union, or of the European Economic Area, or parties to the North American Free Trade Agreement or the European Free Trade Agreement that, in any case, meet the requirements of subparagraph b), or any combination thereof.

b) For purposes of subparagraph a), a person will be treated as a resident of a Member State of the European Union or of the European Economic Area or party to the North American Free Trade Agreement or the European Free Trade Agreement only if such person:

(i) is a resident of a Contracting State entitled to the benefits of this Convention by reason of subparagraph a), subparagraph b), clause (i) of subparagraph c), or subparagraph d) of paragraph 2; or

(ii) (A) would be entitled to the benefits of a comprehensive income tax convention in force between any Member State of the European Union or of the European Economic Area or party to the North American Free Trade Agreement or the European Free Trade Agreement and the Contracting State from which the benefits of this Convention are claimed, analogous to subparagraph a), subparagraph b), clause (i) of subparagraph c) or subparagraph d) of paragraph 2, provided that if such other convention does not contain a comprehensive limitation on benefits article, the person would be entitled to the benefits of this Convention under subparagraph a), subparagraph b), clause (i) of subparagraph c), or subparagraph d) of paragraph 2 if such person were a resident of one of the Contracting States under Article 4 (Resident) of this Convention; and

(B) with respect to income referred to in Articles 10 (Dividends), 11 (Interest) or 12 (Royalties), would be entitled under the convention referred to in clause (ii) of this subparagraph to a rate of tax with respect to the particular class of income for which benefits are being claimed under this Convention that is at least as low as the rate applicable under this Convention.

4.   a) A resident of a Contracting State will be entitled to benefits of the Convention with respect to an item of income derived from the other State, regardless of whether the resident is entitled to benefits under paragraph 2 or 3 of this Article, if the resident is engaged in the active conduct of a trade or business in the first-mentioned State (other than the business of making or managing investments for the resident's own account, unless these activities are banking, insurance or securities activities carried on by a bank, insurance company or registered securities dealer), and the income derived from the other Contracting State is derived in connection with, or is incidental to, that trade or business and that resident satisfies any other conditions for obtaining such benefits.

b) If the resident or any of its associated enterprises carries on a trade or business activity in the other Contracting State which gives rise to an item of income, subparagraph a) of this paragraph shall apply to such item only if the trade or business activity in the first-mentioned State is substantial in relation to the trade or business activity in the other State. Whether a trade or business activity is substantial for purposes of this paragraph will be determined based on all the facts and circumstances.

c) In determining whether a person is "engaged in the active conduct of a trade or business" in a Contracting State under subparagraph a) of this paragraph, activities conducted by a partnership in which that person is a partner and activities conducted by persons connected to such person shall be deemed to be conducted by such person. A person shall be connected to another if one possesses at least 50 percent of the beneficial interest in the other (or, in the case of a company, at least 50 percent of the aggregate vote and at least 50 percent of the aggregate value of the shares in the company or of the beneficial equity interest in the company) or another person possesses, directly or indirectly, at least 50 percent of the beneficial interest (or, in the case of a company, at least 50 percent of the aggregate vote and at least 50 percent of the aggregate value of the shares in the company or of the beneficial equity interest in the company) in each person. In any case, a person shall be considered to be connected to another if, based on all the relevant facts and circumstances, one has control of the other or both are under the control of the same person or persons.

5. Notwithstanding the preceding provisions of this Article, where an enterprise of a Contracting State derives income from the other Contracting State, and that income is

attributable to a permanent establishment which that enterprise has in a third jurisdiction, the tax benefits that would otherwise apply under the other provisions of the Convention will not apply to any item of income if the combined tax that is actually paid with respect to such income in the first-mentioned State and in the third jurisdiction is less than 60 percent of the tax that would have been payable in the first-mentioned State if the income were earned in that State by the enterprise and were not attributable to the permanent establishment in the third jurisdiction. Any dividends, interest or royalties to which the provisions of this paragraph apply shall be subject to tax at a rate that shall not exceed 15 percent of the gross amount thereof. Any other income to which the provisions of this paragraph apply will be subject to tax under the provisions of the domestic law of the other Contracting State, notwithstanding any other provision of the Convention. The provisions of this paragraph shall not apply if:

> a) in the case of royalties, the royalties are received as compensation for the use of, or the right to use, intangible property produced or developed by the permanent establishment itself; or

> b) in the case of any other income, the income derived from the other Contracting State is derived in connection with, or is incidental to, the active conduct of a trade or business carried on by the permanent establishment in the third jurisdiction (other than the business of making, managing or simply holding investments for the person's own account, unless these activities are banking or securities activities carried on by a bank or registered securities dealer).

6. Notwithstanding the preceding provisions of this Article, if a company that is a resident of a Contracting State, or a company that controls directly or indirectly such a company, has outstanding a class of shares:

> a) which is subject to terms or other arrangements which entitle its holders to a portion of the income of the company derived from the other Contracting State that is larger than the portion such holders would receive absent such terms or arrangements ("the disproportionate part of the income"); and

> b) 50 percent or more of which is owned by persons who are not entitled to benefits under paragraph 2 of this Article;

the benefits of this Convention shall not apply to the disproportionate part of the income.

7. A resident of a Contracting State that is not entitled to benefits pursuant to the preceding paragraphs of this Article shall, nevertheless, be granted benefits of the Convention if the competent authority of the other Contracting State determines that the establishment, acquisition or maintenance of such person and the conduct of its operations did not have as one of its principal purposes the obtaining of benefits under the Convention. The competent authority of the other Contracting State shall consult with the competent authority of the first-mentioned State before denying the benefits of the Convention under this paragraph.

8. a) For purposes of this Article the term "principal class of shares" means the ordinary or common shares of the company, provided that such class of shares

represents the majority of the voting power and value of the company. If no single class of ordinary or common shares represents the majority of the aggregate voting power and value of the company, the "principal class of shares" is that class or those classes that in the aggregate represent a majority of the aggregate voting power and value of the company.

b) For purposes of this Article the term "recognized stock exchange" means:

(i) the NASDAQ System owned by the National Association of Securities Dealers, Inc. and any stock exchange registered with the U.S. Securities and Exchange Commission as a national securities exchange under the U.S. Securities Exchange Act of 1934;

(ii) the Icelandic Stock Exchange;

(iii) the stock exchanges of Amsterdam, Brussels, Copenhagen, Frankfurt, Hamburg, Helsinki, London, Oslo, Paris, Stockholm, Sydney, Tokyo, and Toronto; and

(iv) any other stock exchange agreed upon by the competent authorities of both Contracting States.

c)   For purposes of this Article a company's primary place of management and control will be in the State of which it is a resident only if executive officers and senior management employees exercise day-to-day responsibility for more of the strategic, financial and operational policy decision making for the company (including its direct and indirect subsidiaries) in that State than in any other state, and the staffs conduct more of the day-to-day activities necessary for preparing and making those decisions in that State than in any other state.

ARTICLE 22
Relief from Double Taxation

1. In accordance with the provisions and subject to the limitations of the law of the United States (as it may be amended from time to time without changing the general principle hereof), the United States shall allow to a resident or citizen of the United States as a credit against the United States tax on income:

a) the income tax paid or accrued to Iceland on behalf of such citizen or resident; and

b) in the case of a United States company owning at least 10 percent of the voting stock of a company that is a resident of Iceland and from which the United States company receives dividends, the income tax paid or accrued to Iceland by or on behalf of the payer with respect to the profits out of which the dividends are paid.

For the purposes of this paragraph, the taxes referred to in subparagraph a) of paragraph 3 and paragraph 4 of Article 2 (Taxes Covered) shall be considered income taxes.

2. For the purposes of applying paragraph 1 of this Article,

    a) subject to subparagraph b) of this paragraph, an item of gross income, as determined under the laws of the United States, derived by a resident of the United States that, under this Convention, may be taxed in Iceland shall be deemed to be income from sources in Iceland;

    b) however, gains derived by an individual while that individual was a resident of the United States, that are taxed by the United States in accordance with the Convention, and that may also be taxed in Iceland by reason only of paragraph 5 of Article 13 (Capital Gains), shall be deemed to be gains from sources in the United States.

3. In the case of Iceland, double taxation shall be avoided as follows:

    a) When a resident of Iceland derives income which, in accordance with the provisions of this Convention, may be taxed in the United States, Iceland shall allow as a deduction from the tax on the income of that resident an amount equal to the income tax paid in the United States;

    b) Such deduction shall not, however, exceed that part of the income tax, as computed before the deduction is given, which is attributable to the income that may be taxed in the United States;

    c) When a resident of Iceland derives income which, in accordance with the provisions of this Convention, shall be taxable only in the United States, Iceland may include this income in the tax base but shall allow as a deduction from income tax that part of the income tax which is attributable to the income derived from the United States.

For the purposes of this paragraph, the United States taxes referred to in subparagraph b) of paragraph 3 and paragraph 4 of Article 2 (Taxes Covered) shall be considered income taxes, and shall be allowed as a deduction against the Icelandic tax on income.

4. Where a United States citizen is a resident of Iceland:

    a) with respect to items of income that under the provisions of this Convention are exempt from United States tax or that are subject to a reduced rate of United States tax when derived by a resident of Iceland who is not a United States citizen, Iceland shall allow as a credit against Icelandic tax, only the tax paid, if any, that the United States may impose under the provisions of this Convention, other than taxes that may be imposed solely by reason of citizenship under the saving clause of paragraph 4 of Article 1 (General Scope);

    b) for purposes of computing United States tax on those items of income referred to in subparagraph a), the United States shall allow as a credit against United States tax the income tax paid to Iceland after the credit referred to in subparagraph a); the credit so allowed shall not reduce the portion of the United States tax that is creditable against the Icelandic tax in accordance with subparagraph a); and

c) for the exclusive purpose of relieving double taxation in the United States under subparagraph b), items of income referred to in subparagraph a) shall be deemed to arise in Iceland to the extent necessary to avoid double taxation of such income under subparagraph b).

ARTICLE 23
Non-Discrimination

1. Nationals of a Contracting State shall not be subjected in the other Contracting State to any taxation or any requirement connected therewith, which is other or more burdensome than the taxation and connected requirements to which nationals of that other State in the same circumstances, in particular with respect to residence, are or may be subjected. This provision shall, notwithstanding the provisions of Article 1 (General Scope), also apply to persons who are not residents of one or both of the Contracting States. However, for the purposes of United States taxation, United States nationals who are subject to tax on a worldwide basis are not in the same circumstances as nationals of Iceland who are not residents of the United States.

2. The taxation on a permanent establishment which an enterprise of a Contracting State has in the other Contracting State shall not be less favourably levied in that other State than the taxation levied on enterprises of that other State carrying on the same activities. This provision shall not be construed as obliging a Contracting State to grant to residents of the other Contracting State any personal allowances, reliefs and reductions for taxation purposes on account of civil status or family responsibilities which it grants to its own residents.

3. Except where the provisions of paragraph 1 of Article 9 (Associated Enterprises), paragraph 4 of Article 11 (Interest), or paragraph 6 of Article 12 (Royalties), apply, interest, royalties and other disbursements paid by an enterprise of a Contracting State to a resident of the other Contracting State shall, for the purpose of determining the taxable profits of such enterprise, be deductible under the same conditions as if they had been paid to a resident of the first-mentioned State. Similarly, any debts of an enterprise of a Contracting State to a resident of the other Contracting State shall, for the purpose of determining the taxable capital of such enterprise, be deductible under the same conditions as if they had been contracted to a resident of the first-mentioned State.

4. Enterprises of a Contracting State, the capital of which is wholly or partly owned or controlled, directly or indirectly, by one or more residents of the other Contracting State, shall not be subjected in the first-mentioned State to any taxation or any requirement connected therewith which is other or more burdensome than the taxation and connected requirements to which other similar enterprises of the first-mentioned State are or may be subjected.

5. Nothing in this Article shall be construed as preventing either Contracting State from imposing a tax as described in paragraph 8 of Article 10 (Dividends).

6. The provisions of this Article shall, notwithstanding the provisions of Article 2 (Taxes Covered), apply to taxes of every kind and description imposed by a Contracting State or a political subdivision or local authority thereof.

ARTICLE 24
Mutual Agreement Procedure

1. Where a person considers that the actions of one or both of the Contracting States result or will result for him in taxation not in accordance with the provisions of this Convention, he may, irrespective of the remedies provided by the domestic law of those States, and the time limits prescribed in such laws for presenting claims for refunds, present his case to the competent authority of either State.

2. The competent authority shall endeavor, if the objection appears to it to be justified and if it is not itself able to arrive at a satisfactory solution, to resolve the case by mutual agreement with the competent authority of the other Contracting State, with a view to the avoidance of taxation which is not in accordance with the Convention. Any agreement reached shall be implemented notwithstanding any time limits or other procedural limitations in the domestic law of the Contracting States.

3. The competent authorities of the Contracting States shall endeavor to resolve by mutual agreement any difficulties or doubts arising as to the interpretation or application of the Convention. In particular the competent authorities of the Contracting States may agree:

a) to the same attribution of income, deductions, credits, or allowances of an enterprise of a Contracting State to its permanent establishment situated in the other Contracting State;

b) to the same allocation of income, deductions, credits, or allowances between persons;

c) to the same characterization of particular items of income, including the same characterization of income that is assimilated to income from shares by the taxation law of one of the Contracting States and that is treated as a different class of income in the other State;

d) to the same characterization of persons;

e) to the same application of source rules with respect to particular items of income;

f) to a common meaning of a term; and

g) to the application of the provisions of domestic law regarding penalties, fines, and interest in a manner consistent with the purposes of the Convention.

They may also consult together for the elimination of double taxation in cases not provided for in the Convention.

4. The competent authorities of the Contracting States may communicate with each other directly, for the purpose of reaching an agreement in the sense of the preceding paragraphs.

ARTICLE 25
Exchange of Information and Administrative Assistance

1. The competent authorities of the Contracting States shall exchange such information as is relevant for carrying out the provisions of this Convention or of the domestic laws concerning taxes of every kind imposed by a Contracting States, insofar as the taxation thereunder is not contrary to the Convention including information relating to the assessment or collection of, the enforcement or prosecution in respect of, or the determination of appeals in relation to, the taxes covered by the Convention. The exchange of information is not restricted by paragraph 1 of Article 1 (General Scope) and Article 2 (Taxes Covered). Any information received by a Contracting State shall be treated as secret in the same manner as information obtained under the domestic laws of that State and shall be disclosed only to persons or authorities (including courts and administrative bodies) involved in the assessment, collection or administration of, the enforcement or prosecution in respect of, or the determination of appeals in relation to the taxes referred to above, or the oversight of the above. Such persons or authorities shall use the information only for such purposes. They may disclose the information in public court proceedings or in judicial decisions.

2. If information is requested by a Contracting State in accordance with this Article, the other Contracting State shall obtain that information in the same manner and to the same extent as if the tax of the first-mentioned State were the tax of that other State and were being imposed by that other State, notwithstanding that the other State may not, at that time, need such information for purposes of its own tax.

3. In no case shall the provisions of paragraphs 1 and 2 be construed so as to impose on a Contracting State the obligation:

      a) to carry out administrative measures at variance with the laws and administrative practice of that or of the other Contracting State;

      b) to supply information which is not obtainable under the laws or in the normal course of the administration of that or of the other Contracting State;

      c) to supply information which would disclose any trade, business, industrial, commercial or professional secret or trade process, or information, the disclosure of which would be contrary to public policy (ordre public).

4. If specifically requested by the competent authority of a Contracting State, the competent authority of the other Contracting State shall provide information under this Article in the form of depositions of witnesses and authenticated copies of unedited original documents (including books, papers, statements, records, accounts, and writings), to the same extent such

depositions and documents can be obtained under the laws and administrative practices of that other State with respect to its own taxes.

5. Each of the Contracting States shall endeavor to collect on behalf of the other Contracting State such amounts as may be necessary to ensure that relief granted by the Convention from taxation imposed by that other State does not inure to the benefit of persons not entitled thereto. This paragraph shall not impose upon either of the Contracting States the obligation to carry out administrative measures that would be contrary to its sovereignty, security, or public policy.

6. The competent authority of a Contracting State intending to send officials of that State to the other Contracting State to interview individuals and examine books and records with the consent of the persons subject to examination shall notify the competent authority of the other Contracting State of that intention.

ARTICLE 26
Members of Diplomatic Missions and Consular Posts

Nothing in this Convention shall affect the fiscal privileges of members of diplomatic missions or consular posts under the general rules of international law or under the provisions of special agreements.

ARTICLE 27
Entry Into Force

1. This Convention shall be subject to ratification in accordance with the applicable procedures of each Contracting State. The Contracting States shall notify each other in writing, through diplomatic channels, when their respective applicable procedures have been satisfied.

2. The Convention shall enter into force on the date of the later of the notifications referred to in paragraph 1, and its provisions shall have effect in both Contracting States:

a) in respect of taxes withheld at source, on income derived on or after 1 January in the calendar year next following the year in which the Convention enters into force;

b) in respect of other taxes, for taxes chargeable for any tax year beginning on or after 1 January in the calendar year next following the year in which the Convention enters into force.

3. The Convention between the United States of America and the Republic of Iceland for the Avoidance of Double Taxation and the Prevention of Fiscal Evasion with Respect to Taxes on Income and Capital, signed May 7, 1975, ("the prior Convention") shall cease to have effect in relation to any tax from the date on which this Convention has effect in relation to that tax in accordance with paragraph 2 of this Article. Notwithstanding the preceding sentence,

where any person entitled to benefits under the prior Convention would have been entitled to greater benefits thereunder than under this Convention, the prior Convention shall, at the election of such person, continue to have effect in its entirety with respect to such person for a twelve-month period from the date on which the provisions of this Convention otherwise would have effect under paragraph 2 of this Article. The prior Convention shall terminate on the last date on which it has effect in relation to any tax in accordance with the foregoing provisions of this paragraph.

4. Notwithstanding the entry into force of this Convention, an individual who was entitled to benefits of Article 21 (Teachers) of the prior Convention at the time of the entry into force of this Convention shall continue to be entitled to such benefits until such time as the individual would cease to be entitled to benefits if the prior Convention remained in force.

ARTICLE 28

Termination

This Convention shall remain in force until terminated by a Contracting State. Either Contracting State may terminate the Convention, through diplomatic channels, by giving notice of termination in writing at least six months before the end of any calendar year. In such event, the Convention shall cease to have effect in both Contracting States:

a) in respect of taxes withheld at source, on income derived on or after 1 January in the calendar year next following the year in which the notice is given;

b) in respect of other taxes, for taxes chargeable for any tax year beginning on or after 1 January in the calendar year next following the year in which the notice is given.

IN WITNESS WHEREOF the undersigned, being duly authorized thereto by their respective Governments, have signed this Convention.

Done in duplicate at Washington on this twenty-third day of October 2007, in the English and Icelandic languages, both texts being equally authentic.

FOR THE GOVERNMENT OF   FOR THE GOVERNMENT OF
THE UNITED STATES OF AMERICA: ICELAND:

Protocol

At the signing of the Convention concluded today between the Government of the United States of America and the Government of Iceland for the Avoidance of Double Taxation and the Prevention of Fiscal Evasion with Respect to Taxes on Income, the undersigned have agreed upon the following additional provisions which shall form an integral part of the said Convention.

1. With reference to Article 3 (General Definitions)

The following shall be considered to meet the requirements of subparagraph l) of paragraph 1:
a) in Iceland: any pension fund or pension plan qualified under the Pension Act or any identical or substantially similar schemes which are created under any law enacted after the signature of the Convention.

b) in the United States, qualified plans under section 401(a) of the Internal Revenue Code, individual retirement plans (including individual retirement plans that are part of a simplified employee pension plan that satisfies section 408(k), individual retirement accounts, individual retirement annuities, section 408(p) accounts, and Roth IRAs under section 408A), section 457(g) governmental plans, section 403(a) qualified annuity plans, and section 403(b) plans, or any identical or substantially similar schemes which are created under any law enacted after the signature of the Convention.

2. With reference to Article 7 (Business Profits)
The principles of the OECD Transfer Pricing Guidelines shall apply, by analogy, for the purposes of determining the profits attributable to a permanent establishment. Accordingly, any of the methods described therein, including profits methods, may be used to determine the income of a permanent establishment so long as those methods are applied in accordance with the Guidelines.

3. Articles 7 (Business Profits) and 23 (Non-Discrimination) shall not prevent Iceland from continuing to tax permanent establishments of United States insurance companies in accordance with Article 70, paragraph 2, section 3 of the Icelandic Tax Code, nor shall it prevent the United States from continuing to tax permanent establishments of Icelandic insurance companies in accordance with section 842 (b) of the Internal Revenue Code.

4. With reference to paragraphs 8 and 9 of Article 10 (Dividends)

The general principle of the "dividend equivalent amount", as used in United States law, is to approximate that portion of the income mentioned in paragraph 7 of Article 10 that is comparable to the amount that would be distributed as a dividend if such income were earned by a subsidiary incorporated in the United States. For any year, a foreign corporation's dividend equivalent amount is equal to the after-tax earnings attributable to the foreign corporation's (i) income attributable to a permanent establishment in the United States, (ii) income from real property in the United States that is taxed on a net basis under Article 6 (Income from Immovable Property (Real Property)), and (iii) gain from a real property interest taxable by the United States under paragraph 1 of Article 13 (Capital Gains), reduced by any increase in the foreign corporation's net investment in U.S. assets or increased by any reduction in the foreign corporation's net investment in U.S. assets.

5. With reference to Article 16 (Artistes and Sportsmen)

Nothing shall preclude a Contracting State from withholding tax from such payments according to its domestic laws. However, if according to the provisions of this Article, such remuneration or income may only be taxed in the other Contracting State, the first-mentioned Contracting State shall make a refund of the tax so withheld upon a duly filed claim. Such claim must be filed with the tax authorities that have collected the withholding tax within five years after the close of the calendar year in which the tax was withheld.

6.   With reference to Article 21 (Limitation on Benefits)

The competent authorities of the Contracting States shall consult together with a view to developing a commonly agreed application of the provisions of this Article. The competent authorities shall, in accordance with the provisions of Article 25 (Exchange of Information and Administrative Assistance), exchange such information as is necessary for carrying out the provisions of this Article.

7. With reference to Article 25 (Exchange of Information and Administrative Assistance)

The powers of each Contracting State's competent authority to obtain information include powers to obtain information held by financial institutions, nominees, or persons acting in an agency or fiduciary capacity (not including information that would reveal confidential communications between a client and an attorney, solicitor or other legal representative, where the client seeks legal advice), and information relating to the ownership of legal persons, and that each Contracting State's competent authority are able to exchange such information in accordance with the Article.

IN WITNESS WHEREOF the undersigned, being duly authorized thereto by their respective Governments, have signed this Protocol.

Done in duplicate at Washington on this twenty-third day of October 2007 in the English and Icelandic languages, both texts being equally authentic.

FOR THE GOVERNMENT OF   **FOR THE GOVERNMENT OF**
THE UNITED STATES OF AMERICA: **ICELAND:**

www.ingramcontent.com/pod-product-compliance
Lightning Source LLC
Chambersburg PA
CBHW060444290526
45793CB00002B/574